CHILDREN IN CRISIS

Living as a Refugee in America

Mohammed's Story

Helen Howard

WORLD ALMANAC® LIBRARY

Please visit our web site at: www.worldalmanaclibrary.com
For a free color catalog describing World Almanac® Library's list of high-quality books
and multimedia programs, call 1-800-848-2928 (USA) or 1-800-387-3178 (Canada).
World Almanac® Library's fax: (414) 332-3567.

Library of Congress Cataloging-in-Publication Data

Howard, Helen.
    Living as a refugee in America: Mohammed's story / by Helen Howard.
      p. cm. — (Children in crisis)
    Includes bibliographical references and index.
    ISBN 0-8368-5959-6 (lib. bdg.)
    1. Nazari, Mohammed—Juvenile literature. 2. Afghan Americans—Biography—Juvenile
literature. 3. Refugee children—United States—Biography—Juvenile literature. 4. Refugees—
United States—Biography—Juvenile literature. 5. Nazari, Mohammed—Interviews—Juvenile
literature. 6. Afghanistan—Social conditions—Juvenile literature. I. Title. II. Children in
crisis (Milwaukee, Wis.)
    E184.A23H69   2005
    973'.086'91409581—dc22   2005045251

This North American edition first published in 2006 by
World Almanac® Library
A Member of the WRC Media Family of Companies
330 West Olive Street, Suite 100
Milwaukee, WI 53212 USA

This U.S. edition copyright © 2006 by World Almanac® Library. Original edition copyright © 2005 by
ticktock Entertainment Ltd. First published in 2005 by ticktock Media Ltd, Unit 2, Orchard Business
Centre, North Farm Road, Tunbridge Wells, Kent TN2 3XF, U.K.

World Almanac® Library editor: Alan Wachtel
World Almanac® Library managing editor: Valerie J. Weber
World Almanac® Library art direction: Tammy West
World Almanac® Library cover design and layout: Dave Kowalski
World Almanac® Library production: Jessica Morris

Photo credits: (t=top; b=bottom; c=center; l=left; r=right): CORBIS: 4, 7, 15, 19b, 21, 4, 29t, 29b, 31r, 40b, 40t, 41, 44.
Exile Images: 9t, 9b, 11, 20, 33t, 44b, 45. International Institute: 39t. Nazari Family: 10t. Stephanie Cordle: 1, 3, 8, 10b, 12,
14, 16, 18, 19l, 22, 34 25l, 25r, 26,27t, 27b, 28, 30l, 13l, 32, 34, 35t, 36, 37l, 38. World Images library: 5, 13l, 13r, 17t,
17b, 23t, 23b, 31, 33b, 35b, 37, 39b, 42, 43l, 43r.

Printed in the United States of America

1 2 3 4 5 6 7 8 9 09 08 07 06 05

The Interviewer

The interviews with Mohammed (the subject of the book) were conducted by Amy De Leal. Amy is a therapist with the International Institute in St. Louis. The International Institute helps refugees and immigrants to the United States achieve independence by teaching English, helping them find jobs, and providing adjustment services that help them to overcome language and cultural barriers.

How Mohammed Was Chosen

Amy says: *"I chose to ask Mohammed to be involved in this book based on his experiences as a refugee. Due to the circumstances the family endured after the disappearance of Mohammed's father and the general conditions in Afghanistan at the time they lived there, the family fled to Iran. Mohammed and his family lived as refugees in Iran and Turkey before coming to the United States. They now live in St. Louis, Missouri. As a result of safety concerns and the need to help care for his younger brother and sister, Mohammed does not have many opportunities to socialize with people his own age outside of school. However, he does get to meet teenagers of a variety of nationalities when he visits the International Institute."*

The Interview Process

Amy says: *"The interview took place at the International Institute of St. Louis. Mohammed and I sat down and talked during one session that lasted approximately two-and-one-half hours. Mohammed and I both felt that it would be better for him to tell his story in one session. Mohammed said he felt very comfortable relating his experiences as a refugee. He was excited about sharing his story and is proud of what he has been able to achieve despite the difficult circumstances he has had to face."*

Amy De Leal (left) poses with the subject of the book, Mohammed Nazari.

CONTENTS

Introduction

At any one time, about thirty-five million people world-wide live in exile from their lands of origin. They are driven from their homes by a natural disaster or by a political, military, or social situation that has endangered or threatens to endanger their lives. When they move to new countries, these people are often classified as refugees. Adjusting to a new country and a new culture is not easy.

WHAT EXACTLY IS A REFUGEE?

Refugees are people who are forced to leave their homes and seek safety outside of their own countries. Reasons that they leave their countries can be anything from war, persecution, or government oppression to natural disasters or famine. Some refugees escape on foot to refugee camps outside the borders of their country. Others travel by boat or airplane to the other side of the world.

People flee from their countries because they are seeking safety and protection. In some more privileged countries, governments have set up programs to help refugees to leave their old country and settle in new countries. There are also many international nongovernmental organizations that assist refugees. Sometimes, however, people resort to illegal methods of escaping their strife-ridden homelands if they are desperate and there seems to be no other way out.

THE HISTORY OF REFUGEES

As long as there has been war and famine, there has been a need for some human beings to flee their home countries in search of safer territories where they can be assured the basic necessities of life. The word *refugee* originated in 1573. It was first used to describe the Calvinists who fled to France to escape political repression in the Spanish-controlled Netherlands.

THE RIGHTS OF REFUGEES

Most countries are required to offer refugees protection, basic human rights, and equal access to public services, in accordance with the Universal Declaration of Human Rights of 1948

Afghanistan is one of many countries in which a political situation has produced refugees.

Top Ten Major Refugee Populations Worldwide*

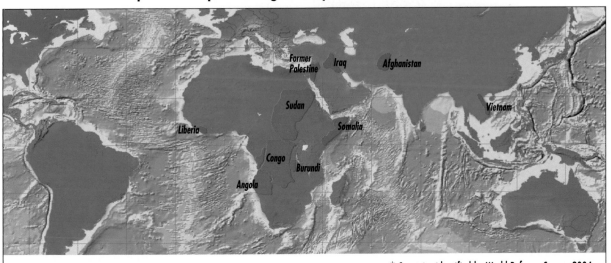

The burka is the head-to-toe covering that many Afghan women wear in public.

Number of People Currently Living as Refugees Worldwide*	
Afghan	**2,136,000**
Sudanese	**606,200**
Iraqi	**600,000**
Burundian	**531,600**
Congolese	**530,400**
Palestinian	**427,900**
Somalian	**402,200**
Vietnamese	**363,200**
Liberian	**353,300**
Angolan	**329,600**

*** Statistics from World Refugee Survey 2004***

and the Geneva Convention of 1951. These international laws state that countries are obligated to accept asylum seekers who are in danger of persecution on the basis of race, social group, religion, or political affiliation. One of the most basic human rights that should be available to refugees and migrants is the right of non-discrimination. This right should entitle refugees to equal opportunities in employment, housing, and governments benefits without their being judged on the basis of their nationality or refugee status. However, this is not always the reality.

A mountainous, landlocked country, Afghanistan has been the scene of many wars.

AFGHANISTAN : A BRIEF HISTORY

The location of Afghanistan at the crossroads of central, western, and southern Asia has made it a territory that different empires have invaded and fought over for more than two thousand years. War has continued almost constantly in Afghanistan over the centuries. The most recently war there took place in 2001, when the United States invaded it following the September11th terrorist attacks.

Over the centuries, Afghanistan has been controlled by many empires including those of the Persians, the Greeks (led by Alexander the Great), the Arabs, the Turks, the Mongols (led by Genghis Khan), and the British. Finally achieving independence in 1747, Afghanistan's strife did not end there, and wars continued throughout the nineteenth and twentieth centuries.

In 1973, after forty years in power, Afghanistan's King Muhammad Zahir Shah was overthrown by a military coup led by his cousin, Daud Khan, ending 226 years of monarchy. In 1978, another coup put a communist government in power. Soon after that, the Soviet Union invaded Afghanistan and seized power. The Soviet occupation provoked the emergence of a group of Afghan freedom fighters, known as the Mujahideen, who fought against the Soviet army. In 1989, the Soviet troops left Afghanistan.

MUJAHIDEEN AND THE TALIBAN

In 1992, the Mujahideen declared Afghanistan to be an Islamic state. Mujahideen warlords fought each other in an ongoing civil war until 1996, when a militant Islamist group called the Taliban seized power. The Taliban brought some order to a previously chaotic society. However, they imposed a very extreme interpretation of Islam on the country. In spite of the fact that the Taliban successfully reunited most of Afghanistan, civil war still continued in the country. Access to food, clean water, and employment also decreased during Taliban rule. In addition, during this time Afghanistan became the headquarters of al-Qaeda, an Islamist terrorist group.

AFGHANISTAN FACTS AND FIGURES

- *Population: 28 million*

- *Capital city: Kabul*

- *Geography: landlocked, mountainous landscape with some plains*

- *Climate: cold winters and dry, hot summers*

- *Languages: 35 percent Pashtu ; 50 percent Afghan Persian/Dari; 11 percent Turkmen and Uzbek*

- *Religions: 84 percent Sunni Muslim; 15 percent Shi'a Muslim*

The damage to Afghanistan resulting from the U.S.-led invasion in 2001–2002 affected the whole country, and it will take many years for the country to fully recover.

SEPTEMBER 11 AND TERRORISM

When sites in the United States, including the World Trade Center and the Pentagon, were attacked by four hijacked airplanes on September 11, 2001, it was quickly determined that the Islamist terrorist network al-Qaeda, led by Osama bin Laden, was responsible. It was known that the Taliban were harboring the Saudi Arabia-born terrorist leader. When the Taliban refused to hand over bin Laden, the United States organized an international coalition and began a military assault.

By January 2002, the Taliban was defeated and overthrown, and the operations of al-Qaeda were seriously disrupted. Although many al-Qaeda terrorists were killed or captured, many of the organization's leaders and prominent figures—including bin Laden—had gone into hiding. Attacks against the U.S.-led coalition continued, but an interim government supported by the coalition took control of the country, and elections were held in 2004. Since then, Afghanistan has been gradually stabilizing. U.S.-led forces remain in the country, looking for Osama bin Laden.

RECENT HISTORY TIME LINE

1954–1955 Afghanistan is denied military assistance by the United States. The Soviet Union agrees to assist the country instead.

1973 Prince Daud organizes a coup against the monarchy and proclaims Afghanistan a republic and himself as its first president.

1978 A communist group, the Peoples Democratic Party of Afghanistan (PDPA), overthrows President Daud in a coup and assumes power. The people of Afghanistan rebel against the PDPA government.

1979 Forty-five hundred Soviet "advisors" enter Afghanistan to help the PDPA. Afghanistan is declared independent.

1980 The Soviet Union's Red Army engages in a fierce battle with the Mujahideen.

1989 The Soviet army leaves Afghanistan.

1991 The PDPA government falls.

1993 Mujahideen warlords begin a civil war.

1996 The Taliban seizes control of 95 percent of Afghanistan.

2001 The United States is attacked by al-Qaeda, which uses hijacked planes to kill a total of 2,973 people.

LATE-2001 After the Taliban refuses to turn over al-Qaeda leader Osama bin Laden, a U.S. led international coalition attacks the Taliban and al-Qaeda. Hamid Karzai is sworn in as chairman of a six-month, interim Afghan government.

2004 Afghanistan holds its first democratic elections. Hamid Karzai wins.

CHAPTER ONE: Meet Mohammed

More than three million refugees have returned home to Afghanistan since the fall of the Taliban in late 2001. Millions of Afghans, however, still remain outside their homeland. Many live in poverty in refugee camps in Iran and Pakistan. Other refugees, like Mohammed Nazari and his family, have settled permanently in the United States.

MOHAMMED SAYS:

"My name is Mohammed Nazari, and I am fifteen years old. I was born in Kabul in Afghanistan. I came to the United States two years ago with my mother, brother, and sister. We did not know where our father was at that time. When we left Afghanistan, I was really young—about six or seven years old. First of all, our family went to Pakistan, but we only lived there for one month. Then we moved to Tehran, the capital city of Iran, where we lived for two years. After that, we lived in Turkey for two years and then we eventually moved to America.

Fifteen-year-old Mohammed Nazari is happy to be living in the United States after a long journey through many countries.

I am the sort of person who likes to know about everything—I like to learn new things and learn all about different places all over the world. I speak four different languages: Iranian, Farsi, Turkish, and English. I like to think I have a strong character and that I will always be around to help other people when they need me to. I like playing video games and I usually play these games at home with my brother and sister. I like pop music—mainly Iranian stuff like The Black Cats and Sandy. I also like sports, and I am especially good at soccer."

Many refugees, such as these Afghans in Peshawar, Pakistan, are forced to live in refugee camps.

BECOMING A REFUGEE

There are several ways of becoming a refugee. People can apply for refugee status from their home countries or from countries bordering their own. Refugee status can also be authorized when they arrive in a new country.

Refugees can be admitted to the United States through the Overseas Admissions Program. Staff of U.S.-based nongovernmental organizations and the United Nations' (UN) refugee agency assist U.S. government officers in identifying which refugees are most in need of resettlement.

TEMPORARY HOUSING

Most refugees coming to the United States need to have a contact person or family already living in the country before they can be granted asylum. These people are usually expected to provide housing for the refugees until they can find their own accommodations, although they often have government help. Refugees coming to the United Kingdom (UK) are sometimes held in detention centers or have their housing set up by the government until their asylum applications have been processed. Those who can are allowed to live independently.

The UK's Migrant Helpline is one of many organizations that offer temporary housing to newly arrived refugees.

"My mother and father are both Muslim, and they are both Afghan. They come from different cities to each other. At first, my mother liked somebody else, but he went to Germany and never came back. Then, she met my father, and they started talking and got together and eventually got married.

My brother Mahdi is eleven, and my sister Fereshte is nine years old. My mother, brother, and sister are here with me in America, but our father lives in Greece. When we lived in Afghanistan, my dad worked as an assistant to a truck driver. He used to deliver fruit and other foods to different cities. One day, he went off on a job and didn't come back. We waited and waited, and two years went by, and he still didn't come back.

This is Mohammed's uncle, who is one of a small number of Mohammed's extended family still living in Afghanistan.

Family mealtimes in the Nazari household are opportunities to eat traditional Afghan foods.

One day my father's friend said to us, 'Maybe he's dead or he's not going to come back, and if you guys want, I can take you to Iran. You can sell all your stuff, like your house, and I can take you guys with the money.' We didn't want to leave without our father, but we were so desperate to leave that we really had no choice.

Eventually, we found out that our father wasn't dead but living in Greece. He doesn't have a house there—he just stays at the park. He always says how cold it is out there and that he cannot sleep on the ground. He tries to find work, but they don't give him any work, because he has a kidney problem, and the doctor says he cannot work."

REFUGEES: THE CHANGING FIGURE

The U.S. target for resettling refugees was seventy thousand a year for most of the 1990s. After September 11, 2001, the United States—and much of the Western world—introduced more rigorous security checks on refugee applicants. This slowed entries so much that only twenty-seven thousand of the thousands who applied for refugee status were accepted into the United States in 2002. Since then, systems have begun to run more smoothly, allowing numbers to creep up annually. A total of ninety thousand refugees are expected to settle in the United States in 2005.

The United Nations stated that the total number of people seeking asylum has dropped to the lowest level in seventeen years. This decrease is largely because of the decline in refugees from Iraq and Afghanistan. However, it is also due to the many obstacles placed in the way of refugees by Western countries.

REUNITING FAMILIES

During the desperate ordeal of fleeing a troubled country, families often split up. There are many reasons why this happens, such as male family members going to war and losing contact with their families. Whatever the circumstances, it can be hugely traumatic for the families involved.

After the attacks of September 11, 2001, the number of nationalities eligible for the United States' Family Reunification Program for refugee families was reduced from six in 2002 to four in 2003 because of the number of fraudulent applications. As a result of the introduction of fraud-prevention measures, people from fourteen countries will qualify for the program from 2005.

Refugees can often be separated from family members for long periods. This Afghan family was reunited in Kabul after five years apart.

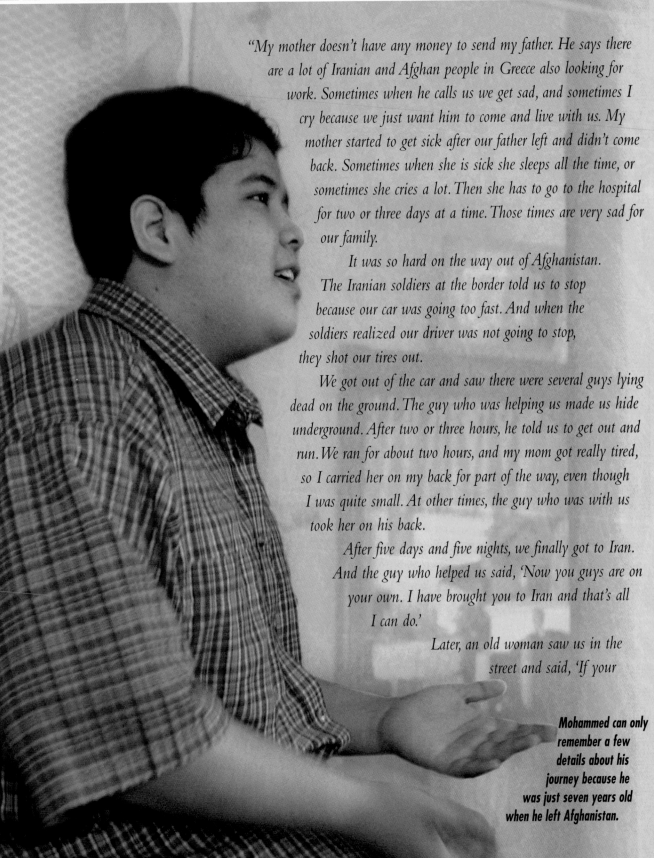

"My mother doesn't have any money to send my father. He says there are a lot of Iranian and Afghan people in Greece also looking for work. Sometimes when he calls us we get sad, and sometimes I cry because we just want him to come and live with us. My mother started to get sick after our father left and didn't come back. Sometimes when she is sick she sleeps all the time, or sometimes she cries a lot. Then she has to go to the hospital for two or three days at a time. Those times are very sad for our family.

It was so hard on the way out of Afghanistan. The Iranian soldiers at the border told us to stop because our car was going too fast. And when the soldiers realized our driver was not going to stop, they shot our tires out.

We got out of the car and saw there were several guys lying dead on the ground. The guy who was helping us made us hide underground. After two or three hours, he told us to get out and run. We ran for about two hours, and my mom got really tired, so I carried her on my back for part of the way, even though I was quite small. At other times, the guy who was with us took her on his back.

After five days and five nights, we finally got to Iran. And the guy who helped us said, 'Now you guys are on your own. I have brought you to Iran and that's all I can do.'

Later, an old woman saw us in the street and said, 'If your

Mohammed can only remember a few details about his journey because he was just seven years old when he left Afghanistan.

mother can work, I will pay her to clean my house.' Her daughter taught us kids Farsi [the language commonly spoken in Iran today]. After the old lady died, the daughter told us she was going to leave Iran. So we sold everything we owned and used the money to get to Turkey. We took a bus that was supposed to take us to Istanbul. Then the guy that organized it and his friend came onto the bus and called themselves police. But they weren't really police—they just wanted to get money from everyone. But nobody gave them any, so they kicked everybody off.

Then, an Afghan guy told us there was an organization called the United Nations and that they would help us go somewhere else. He said everything was expensive in Turkey and that it wasn't a good place for us to be. So he gave us an address and put us on a bus to Ankara [the capital of Turkey]."

Mohammed's bus journey from Iran to Turkey probably took about twenty-four hours.

FACTS: TWO DIFFERENT COUNTRIES

In many ways, life in Afghanistan couldn't be more different than life in the United States. Some of the major differences are:

• Afghanistan is one of the poorest countries in the world. The United States, in contrast, has one of the world's richest economies.

• Under the Taliban, most freedoms were denied to women in Afghanistan. Even after the fall of the Taliban, Afghan women still have lower social status than men. In the United States, however, all people are legally entitled to equal status, regardless of gender, race, or religion. It is important to note, however, that, in spite of laws guaranteeing equal rights, prejudices still exist in the Western world.

• Afghanistan is a developing country that has endured many years of war. As a result, the country's basic infrastructure—including utilities such as electricity, water, and sanitation—is either unavailable or unreliable. In contrast, most people in the United States have the basic resources they need.

• A total of 39 percent of Afghan boys are enrolled in school while, until recently, girls weren't allowed to attend school at all. In the United States, 98 percent of boys and girls go to school.

Compared to people in the United States and other developed nations, most people in Afghanistan are poor.

Mohammed walks to the International Institute with his sister and brother on Saturdays. From there, they catch a bus to the mosque.

"There were some people in Ankara who knew how to speak Farsi. They said, 'How did you get here? Do you have passports?' And we said, 'No. We came secretly, without anything.' And one guy told us that we would have to go to the United Nations office in a different city. There was also a mosque in this city with a small park behind it.

We ended up sleeping in that park until the UN could find us somewhere to live. Every week they would say, 'Come back next Friday,' until one day, we were sent to this old house where four other mothers with no husbands and about seventeen kids lived. One day, this guy told us very quietly, 'Your father's dead. We saw his body.' We said, 'Maybe it was someone else's.' We didn't want to believe it.

After seven or eight months, we were told we had passed, which meant we were allowed to stay in Turkey for longer. We were then sent to another place to live. Here, we tracked down my uncle's phone number in Afghanistan. We called him, and he said, 'No, your father is not dead. He's alive, but we don't know where he is.'

After two years, we were told we had to go to Britain. Then, eventually we were told, 'You cannot go to Britain anymore, America wants the Afghans now.' So the UN educated us about how things would be in America and how we should act when we got there. The first time I went up in an airplane was when we flew from Turkey to the U.S.

Now, I live in the city of St. Louis, in Missouri. It is a good place to live, with friendly people. I have some good friends here. I just think it's a good city because it has a lot of beautiful places—parks and big apartments. It's cool if you see it from the sky."

REFUGEE COMMUNITIES

In the United States, some states have particularly high refugee populations. For example, many Afghan refugees have taken up residence in California, Virginia, Texas, Florida, New York, Massachusetts, Arizona, Georgia, Idaho, Washington, and Missouri. A local community of Afghan people can often help new refugees to settle more quickly.

Organized social and cultural events for refugee communities can also assist in the adjustment process. Many nongovernmental organizations (NGOs) organize such events in their local areas.

A CULTURALLY DIVERSE CITY

St. Louis is a city in the midwestern United States at the center of a metropolitan area that has more than 2.6 million people. With members of more than one hundred different ethnic groups living in and around it, St. Louis is well known for its cultural diversity.

The Gateway Arch in St. Louis, which was completed in 1965, was built to commemorate the westward growth of the United States during the nineteenth century.

"There are a lot of kids in our neighborhood, but I don't go out very often, so I don't really know what's going on out there. During the day, I'm in school and in the house. I only really go out to do the shopping, and sometimes I take my brother and sister out.

I know some of my neighbors. They are nice people. I don't really think there is anything bad about living in America. We feel safe here.

I go to school, where I am in the ninth grade. I can read and write in English, German, and Farsi. The school I go to is an international school. There are a lot of teachers and kids from different countries, like Bosnia, America, Pakistan, and Hindustan. We talk openly about everybody's different cultures quite a lot. My teachers say I am a good student and I am well-behaved in class.

My favorite subject is science, and I also enjoy reading—I have lots of books at home. The teachers are nice to the kids. I didn't go to school in Afghanistan. But I did go for one-and-one-half years in Iran at the first grade, but they took me out because they said, 'You guys don't have passports, so you cannot go to school.' So, then, some Afghans started teaching about twenty kids how to read at home.

My best friends are two Mexican guys, Christian and Victor, and Jafar from Saudi Arabia. We laugh a lot and tell jokes. I don't see them very much because I only have one class with each of them. I don't really hang out with them after school. Last year we had lots of classes together, so we were together a lot, but not this year."

Students from more than thirty different countries attend Soldan International Studies High School, where Mohammed is a student.

SCHOOLING FOR AFGHANS

In 2002, the United Nations estimated that more then 95 percent of Afghan children did not go to school. Since the Taliban were removed from power, however, that figure has improved dramatically. More than three million children have now returned to school in Afghanistan, including one million girls, many of whom had never before seen the inside of a classroom.

In most democratic societies, all children and young people—including refugees—are entitled to free education. For economic reasons, however, the Iranian government has recently ruled to charge Afghan children for their schooling. But many Afghan families simply cannot afford this kind of expense— which equals about U.S. $150 per child—and have chosen to travel back to Afghanistan, even though life there is still very difficult.

In Afghanistan, students often sit two to a desk because schools in the country do not have enough supplies.

EDUCATION FOR REFUGEES

Many young refugees experience bullying and harassment at schools in their new countries. In the UK, United States, and Canada, some schools have introduced anti-bullying programs that include counseling and peer-support for refugees.

In spite of this, school is often a happy place for refugees. A recent survey by Save the Children in the UK found that school was often the highlight of young refugees' lives, particularly if they had come from disrupted backgrounds or had endured traumatic experiences.

Particularly within the last decade, a growing number of secondary schools and independent language schools have designed programs that address the specific needs of older children with little or no knowledge of the English language.

Refugees might experience bullying at school because of their different styles of dress, race, or cultural habits. Many schools have anti-bullying policies.

CHAPTER TWO: Where Is Home?

Many refugees have lived unsettled lives for a long period of time. Often they have traveled through many countries and dangerous situations before reaching their final destinations. Home can mean many places to refugees, some welcoming and others terrifying. No matter how much safer a refugee family might feel when they have settled in their new country, they may still dream of returning to the country from which they came.

The family is important in traditional Afghan culture. Mohammed longs for the day when his father will join the rest of the family in the United States.

Traditional Afghan dress is quite distinctive. Men generally wear loose-fitting long trousers and a shirt, while many Afghan women still wear the traditional blue burka.

MOHAMMED SAYS:

"I don't really remember a lot about living in Afghanistan. I only remember that it wasn't very good. I don't remember what the house we lived in looked like, only that it wasn't a good house. It was always very hot there, and where we lived was very noisy—people shouting and fighting all the time. Here, it is much quieter.

I remember when the Taliban first started taking over. They just forced their way into people's houses and took carpets and things. If people had chickens, cows, or lambs, the Taliban took them. They took everything they could carry—and if it was too heavy, they would come back for it later. They warned us that before they came back next time, everybody had to leave their houses.

So when we knew they were on their way, most people started running. We ran all the way into the mountains so they couldn't see us."

FACTS: LAWS UNDER THE TALIBAN

During the rule of the Taliban, the people of Afghanistan were subjected to a rigorously enforced system of laws. There were often severe punishments if any of the laws were broken. Under the Taliban:

• TV, music, movies, singing, dancing, and alcoholic beverages were all banned.

• Men were forced to wear full, untrimmed beards, and baggy trousers.

• Women were prohibited from working and were not allowed out of the house unless accompanied by a male family member.

• Girls were not allowed to attend school.

• Theft was punished by cutting off the thief's hand.

• Women caught wearing nail polish would have their fingers cut off.

• Individuals who committed adultery would be stoned to death.

• People were imprisoned for not praying five times a day and for not praying at particular times of the day.

• Women who failed to wear the burka—a loose-fitting garment covering the whole body—would be publicly stoned.

During the Taliban years, men who failed to grow long beards were punished with beatings.

19

"But my grandmother and grandfather couldn't walk very far because they were quite old, so they made us leave without them. They said, 'We don't care what happens to us. You guys just go.' So we did, we left, and when we came back we saw that the Taliban had cut my grandmother and grandfather's heads off. The Taliban also sometimes set everything on fire, or they had parties and ate all the food and then just trashed the place and left.

The Taliban killed so many people. When we were living in Turkey, these guys brought around some videos that showed what was going on in Afghanistan. These people back in Afghanistan would send the videos to lots of different places

One of the many things banned by the Taliban were movies. This group of Taliban officials burned hundreds of reels of film in front of downtown Kabul's Zaynab movie theater.

where Afghans lived so that people like us could see what was going on in our country. We watched so many people dying—the videos showed how the people died.

I remember in Afghanistan, all the streets smelled bad. The Taliban would just kill people, and the blood would run like rivers of water. They would take a person and slash their throat and then they would just take another one and do it again.

The Taliban ordered women to stay in the house and do the housework. If they saw a woman outside, they would take her to the soccer stadium—although no one was allowed to play soccer there—then they would shoot her there."

WHO ARE THE TALIBAN?

The Taliban is an Islamist movement that ruled most of Afghanistan from 1996 until 2001. Only three countries (the United Arab Emirates, Pakistan, and Saudi Arabia) officially acknowledged the Taliban as a legitimate government. The Taliban emerged after ongoing rebel wars, and, while they created some stability in Afghanistan after two decades of war and anarchy, their fundamentalist Islamic laws attracted mass criticism. Several years after their defeat in 2001, the remains of the Taliban is now a militia operating in parts of Afghanistan that are outside the control of the government.

OSAMA BIN LADEN AND AL-QAEDA

Al-Qaeda is an international terrorist network. Its goals include ridding Muslim countries of the influence of the West and replacing governments with fundamentalist Islamic regimes. Osama bin Laden is the leader of al-Qaeda and allegedly the man behind the attacks that destroyed the World Trade Center, in New York City; damaged part of the Pentagon, in Washington, D.C.; and crashed an airplane in western Pennsylvania. Bin Laden is still on the run from coalition forces, who continue to hunt for him in Afghanistan and Pakistan.

When it was in power, the Taliban gave al-Qaeda support. Today, although many of its members have been caught, it is thought that al-Qaeda is active around the world.

Osama bin Laden, leader of al-Qaeda, is probably the world's most wanted man. He allegedly admitted responsibility for the September 11, 2001, terrorist attacks.

"And they would make everyone go to the mosque five times a day. Then, even if you went fives times, they would still say, 'Go back!' And we would say, 'We already went five times.' But they would just say, 'What did I say?' And if you said that you wouldn't go, they would just kill you.

Everybody was scared of the Taliban. There was nothing to be happy about when they were in power. You never knew if they were going to come to your house or if they would approach you in the street.

I do miss Afghanistan. I just want to go and see it again. I don't know when that will be. I miss the old houses and friends—mainly the people. But who knows how many of those people are still alive or where they are now?

One of the hardest things about being a refugee is leaving loved ones behind in difficult situations and not knowing whether they are alive or dead.

Day after day we were scared about what was going to happen next when we lived in Afghanistan. One day, one of my friends was playing with this bomb that had fallen down in our neighborhood. He said he didn't think anything was going to happen to him, and he just threw it up in the air, and it came back down and 'BOOM'—it killed him."

More than six years of drought have contributed to severe food and water shortages across Afghanistan.

FAMINE AND POVERTY

As a result of many problems affecting the country—including years of continuous warfare, a harsh, unforgiving climate, and lack of arable land—Afghanistan has been one of the world's poorest, most underdeveloped countries for many years. Following a lengthy period of civil war, droughts, and poor harvests, Afghanistan has endured many years of famine. When the United States invaded Afghanistan in 2001, the country was suffering the worst drought in thirty years.

Today, seven million people are vulnerable to famine, and health-care facilities are not sufficient to deal with the number of malnourished people or those suffering from diseases such as pneumonia, tuberculosis, diarrhea, malaria, and measles.

CHILD SOLDIERS

Many young boys fought against the Soviet invasion of Afghanistan in 1979, and boys were recruited to train as soldiers throughout the remainder of the twentieth century. When the Taliban was in power (1996–2001), there were many reports that boys as young as ten years old were forced to fight. Similarly, the Northern Alliance—which fought against the Taliban—was proven to be using children as young as eleven, in spite of having publicly declared that its soldiers had to be eighteen to join.

During the rule of the Taliban, many boys and young men in Afghanistan were recruited into the army.

"I think we were lucky to get refugee status in America. One day felt like one year in Afghanistan. Nobody was happy there—not happy like we are here. When we left Afghanistan, it was still a long time before we felt safe. We were afraid sometimes when we were in Iran because people kept telling us to leave their country and go home.

When we were in Iran, a lot of the Afghan kids would run wild and fight with each other. They would do things like take some food an old woman was selling and throw it in the street. They would just pick on people like her to prove something—because they would get in serious trouble for fighting with the Iranian boys. I guess they just wanted to show the Iranian guys they could fight.

We were very poor when we lived in Afghanistan. Everybody was. There was not a lot of food for the people and not many stores even if you did have money to buy things you needed. Some people looked for vegetables in the mountains and took them home to eat. So, life in America is much easier.

American people have been welcoming since we got here, and no one in my family has really found it difficult to adjust to life here.

Before, I wanted to go to school, but I didn't go to school in Afghanistan. Then, I only went for one-and-one-half years in Iran and one month in Turkey. Now, I get to go full-time.

When we first got here and we didn't know any English, it was hard getting to know other kids at school.

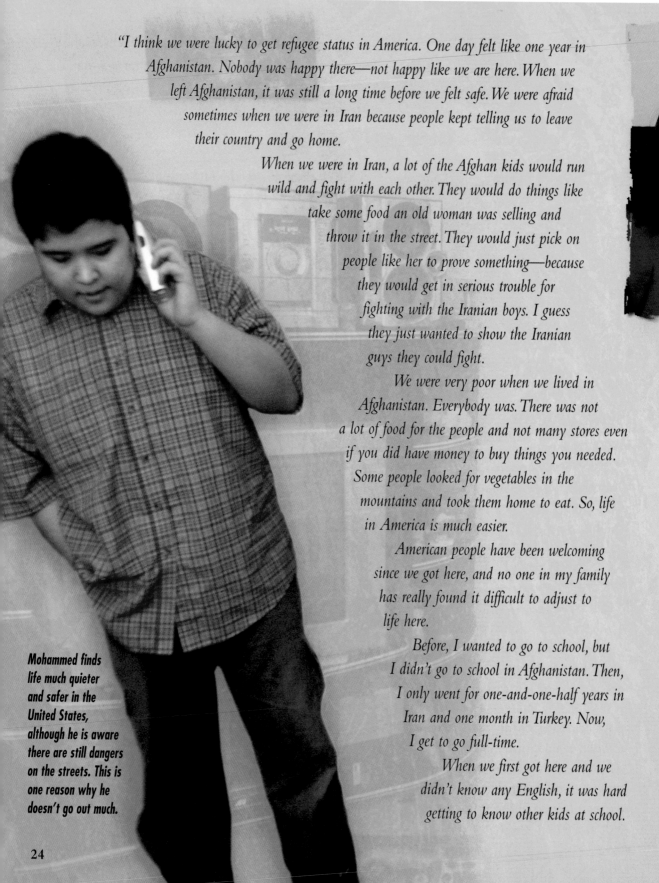

Mohammed finds life much quieter and safer in the United States, although he is aware there are still dangers on the streets. This is one reason why he doesn't go out much.

24

Mohammed is a true friend and role model to his siblings. In addition to walking with them to the bus stop, he also cooks for them when his mother is not well.

But after we learned English, we could understand what the other kids were saying and then we could talk back to them. Basically, if you can't speak English, people aren't going to want to bother with you, are they? But once we could communicate with each other, it was no problem.

Everybody's friendly here. They just say, 'Where you from?' They don't care what country you come from. Most of the people in St. Louis are American, but that doesn't really affect me because I don't spend much time with other people anyway.

The school I go to is a bit different to some schools because it is an international school. Like, my friends are from Mexico and Saudi Arabia and other places."

FACTS: EXPECTATIONS VS. REALITY

For refugees, expectations of their new home country can be romantic and unrealistic. These inaccurate expectations can have a big impact on how they settle into their new life.

• Many refugees expect free health care, such as there is in certain countries. In the UK, for example, health care is free to all residents. In the United States, however, a person must have medical insurance or the ability to pay in cash in order to see a doctor or dentist.

• Some refugees expect to receive disability benefits when they reach the United States because they have high blood pressure or because they consider themselves "too old" to work. Under U.S. law, however, they often do not qualify.

• Some refugees expect to be much better off financially when they reach their new country. Many expect a big house and enough money to buy everything they need. The reality is more often that several family members have to share a bedroom, parents struggle to find work, and families don't have enough money to send children on to higher education.

Mohammed and his family all share the same bedroom. His mother and sister sleep on one side of the room, while the boys sleep on the other.

CHAPTER THREE: Adjusting to a New Life

Moving to a new country as a refugee can be a life-changing experience in many ways. The advantages—including safety, security, food, and freedom—are immediately felt. Some refugees, however, might also experience acute anxiety about the plight of their country and the people they left behind, as well as culture shock when faced with a different and, in many ways, alien way of life. The host country should be prepared to offer newcomers the support they need to adjust.

Mohammed and Mahdi enjoy playing video games—a hobby they would never even have imagined back in Afghanistan—in their spare time.

MOHAMMED SAYS:

"I don't really talk to anyone about how I feel about things. My friends are often busy and want to go and play outside, which I don't really do very often. Also, my mom won't let me hang out with the other Afghan kids in St. Louis. She thinks they just make trouble and are a bad influence on me.

Every day at school, these kids get suspended for five days or something, and when they come back to school, they keep doing the same stuff and getting into the same kind of trouble. They often just skip school. And when the police ask them, 'Why are you guys not in school?,' these kids just tell the policemen that they have dropped out."

Like many refugees who have endured trauma in their home country and the upheaval of moving to a new country, Mohammed's mother suffers from depression.

PSYCHOLOGICAL IMPACT

Afghans are very private people, and they do not generally discuss emotional issues. For this reason, many Afghans with mental-health problems due to traumatic experiences or things they have witnessed find it difficult to engage in the kind of talk therapy common in the West.

The World Health Organization estimates that 95 percent of Afghans have been psychologically affected in some way by the decades of war and violence in Afghanistan. Despite this statistic, there are only four mental-health-care hospitals in the country. Mental-health issues are a growing concern as millions of Afghan refugees are now returning to their homeland.

CULTURE SHOCK

Refugees can also experience culture shock upon arriving in their new country. If they have come from a country where poverty is common and food is scarce, the consumerism and fast-food culture of the West can be a big surprise. In addition, when members of a family speak minimal English, communicating their needs and even such simple tasks as going grocery shopping can be extremely difficult.

Even grocery shopping can be very challenging for refugees who do not know the language and customs of their new country and are not familiar with the products that are available.

"I didn't know much about the U.S. before we moved here. When we arrived we were very happy. It was coming into winter and it started to snow soon after we arrived. That was exciting for my brother and sister because it was the first time they had seen snow. In Turkey and Iran, it got very cold, but there was only ever rain, no snow.

When we grow up, our mom wants us to be doctors or something. She wants to go back to Afghanistan with my father one day, and she hopes we will be able to buy them a house. She says she tries hard to give us what we need and that we should do the same for them when we are grown up. My mother won't learn to drive here or learn English because she is just waiting to go back to Afghanistan. When that happens, I will stay living in the U.S. but will go back to Afghanistan to visit my parents.

I don't feel like I have to marry an Afghan woman. My mother doesn't care who I end up with. I don't even feel that they have to be a Muslim. It would only be important that we belonged to the same faith as each other. If she was Christian, I would become Christian, too, or I would want her to change to be Muslim.

I don't really have an opinion about arranged marriages. I guess I would be fine with it if she was a good lady. But if she was not a nice person, I wouldn't be happy about it.

Afghan women are so much happier now they are free. Now, they can go shopping and go to

Young refugees often find it easier to settle into their new culture than their parents. They generally pick up the new language much faster.

work, or they can go to the park with their children or husbands. Before, under the Taliban, they just had to stay in the house—they couldn't even go to the mosque. Under the Taliban, women in Afghanistan were like birds in cages. I think it is good that men and women in America are equal."

Western sports, such as soccer, and other influences of Western culture were forbidden under the Taliban.

ADOPTING A NEW CULTURE

Many cultural practices in the West must seem completely alien to refugees who have never encountered the Internet, the latest technology, or Western television programs. This is particularly the case for refugees from cultures that have been sheltered from the influences of other countries, as Afghanistan was. Fashions and dating may also be a completely new experience for teenage refugees. In traditional Afghan culture, for example, unmarried girls are not allowed to socialize without their families being present. Yet in the West, it is generally acceptable for young women to socialize independently. Young refugees might be tempted to join their peers who are dating and going to parties, but they may still feel pressure from their families to marry someone from their native culture who has been sheltered from the outside world.

ARRANGED MARRIAGES

Traditionally, young Afghans are told from an early age that their marriage will be arranged for them. In Afghan culture, it is important for family members to uphold their families' "honor," and a child who denies an arranged marriage is likely to be disowned. Statistics show that the divorce rate for arranged marriages is much lower than for marriages chosen by the couple. But research also suggests that, because of pressure from their culture and their families, couples who have had arranged marriages do not even consider divorce an option.

Ritual, ceremony, and family honor are important in traditional Afghan weddings.

"My friends and I ask each other lots of questions about our different cultures. They say, 'What are the presents like there?,' 'What food do you eat there?,' 'What are the people like there?,' and 'What are the soldiers like?'—things like that. And you tell them how it is, and they tell you how it is in their country.

We just ask each other when we want to learn. Friends just want to know about each other and where they have come from. As soon as we got better at English, we all started making lots of friends. I don't really mix with a lot of Afghan guys here. Mainly because my Mom doesn't let me.

I haven't really found it difficult to adjust to life in America. But because we are still learning English, though, sometimes school can be hard. Sometimes, in Social Studies, I get Cs, Ds, or even Fs. Sometimes I have so much homework, I don't know which project to do first! I also have to help my sister and brother with their homework.

I'd like to get a part-time job soon, maybe, like, at Blockbuster, or somewhere else like that. I had a job last summer washing dishes at the bakery store. Every summer the International Institute finds teenagers jobs if they want them. When I first arrived here, I was thirteen, and they told me I was too young to get a summer job.

Mohammed is a dedicated student, although he sometimes finds it difficult to get good grades because English is not his first language.

When I finish school I would like to be a doctor. I like helping people. It is so much harder to find a job in Afghanistan. In Afghanistan, no one would tell me I could be anything I wanted to be when I grew up. But in America, people tell you to follow your dreams and that you can take up any career you want.

I don't really stay that informed about what is happening in Afghanistan, although sometimes I watch the news on TV. When I hear that things are difficult there, it makes me sad. We wish other Afghans could get out of there like we have—that they could be free like us."

On top of his own ever-increasing load of homework, Mohammed also helps his younger brother and sister with their homework.

FACTS: PREJUDICE AND DISCRIMINATION

Refugees often encounter prejudice when settling in a new country. This prejudice can be on the grounds of race, ethnic origin, religion, or refugee status, and it can take many forms.

• Refugees, like many minority groups, may experience discrimination in the workplace, when looking for housing, and when using public services and facilities. This discrimination can involve harassment, vilification, and sometimes actual violence.

• Some sectors of the media and even certain politicians have described asylum seekers and refugees as "invaders" and "illegal immigrants."

• After the September 11th terrorist attacks, there were cases reported in the United States of Arab-American organizations, Islamic centers, and mosques being harassed or vandalized.

• In 2004, the French government passed a controversial law banning the wearing of religious clothing and symbols by school students. Some believe this law will encourage ethnic minorities to integrate more into French society. Others believe it violates the right to freedom of religious expression.

A recent law in France has been criticized for compromising freedom of religious expression by not allowing students to wear clothing required by their religions.

CHAPTER FOUR: Afghan or American?

Once the initial hurdles of settling into a new country are overcome, refugees still have much to get used to. Some want to blend in with the crowd, keeping their religion and heritage private, while others prefer to maintain their traditional ways of doing certain things. Although their new home might seem strange at first, many refugees come to accept and even appreciate belonging to two cultures.

MOHAMMED SAYS:

"My family are Shi'ite Muslim. I think we come from the Tajik tribe, but I am not sure. The traditional Afghan festivals my family celebrates are Nawruz [the first day of the Afghan solar calendar] and Eid, which comes after Ramadan. Although my family are Muslim, we are not orthodox. We practice our religion by copying what our mother does. We go to mosque to pray on Saturdays. They don't have an Afghan mosque in our neighborhood. There's a Pakistani one, but they are mad. We tried to go there, but they changed the locks twice so we couldn't get in. But it beats being in Afghanistan, because there we would have to put up with killing and fighting."

Mohammed's family takes the bus in order to get to a mosque.

ISLAMIC CENTER / MASJID
3843 WEST PINE
ISLAMIC FOUNDATION
EST. 1974

Many Muslims attend regular prayer sessions at a mosque, such as the one shown above.

THE RELIGIONS OF AFGHANISTAN

While Islam is by far the dominant religion in Afghanistan, where 99 percent of the population follows it, other religions exist alongside it, including Christianity, Hinduism, Judaism, Buddhism, and the Baha'i faith. Islam was founded by Muhammad, a prophet, in the seventh century and today has 935 million followers worldwide.

A person who belongs to the Islamic faith is called a Muslim, and there are two major groups of Muslims. Sunni Muslims make up about 85 percent of the world's Muslims, while Shi'a, or Shi'ite, Muslims account for about 15 percent. Muslims worship at a temple called a mosque. They believe there is one true god—Allah—and they believe his "eternal word" is written in a book called the Qur'an. Orthodox muslims are required to perform regular acts of worship, including praying five times a day.

MUSLIM FESTIVALS

ASHURA: the most important period for Shi'ite Muslims, which occurs during the first ten days of the new year.

RAMADAN: the ninth month of the Muslim calendar, during which Muslims fast during the day and visit family in the evenings.

EID UL-FITR: a three-day feast that occurs after the fasting month of Ramadan.

EID UL-ADHA: a three-day feast that concludes with an annual pilgrimage to Mecca, in Saudi Arabia.

Thousands of Muslims flock to Mecca during Eid Ul-Adha to visit the holiest Muslim shrine, the Ka'aba.

33

Living as a Refugee in America

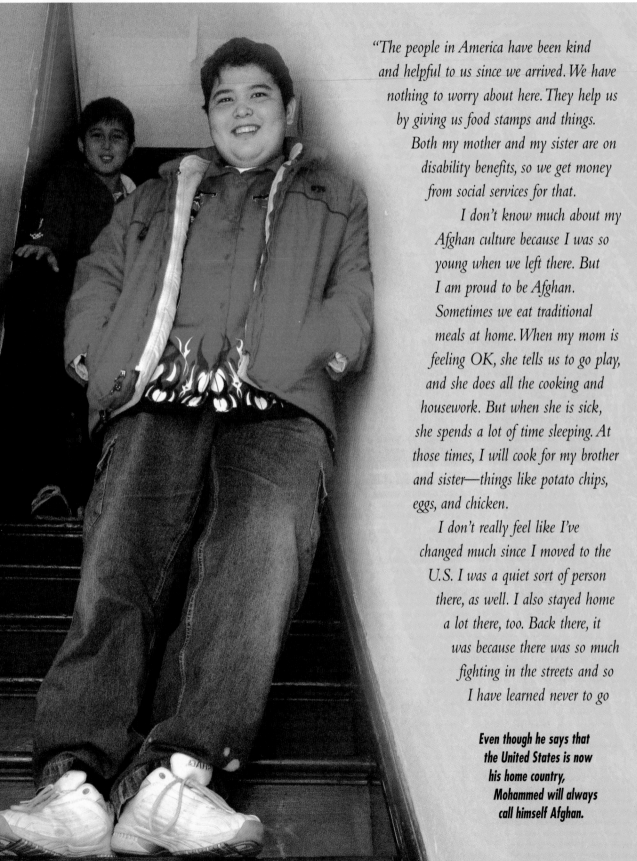

"The people in America have been kind and helpful to us since we arrived. We have nothing to worry about here. They help us by giving us food stamps and things. Both my mother and my sister are on disability benefits, so we get money from social services for that.

I don't know much about my Afghan culture because I was so young when we left there. But I am proud to be Afghan. Sometimes we eat traditional meals at home. When my mom is feeling OK, she tells us to go play, and she does all the cooking and housework. But when she is sick, she spends a lot of time sleeping. At those times, I will cook for my brother and sister—things like potato chips, eggs, and chicken.

I don't really feel like I've changed much since I moved to the U.S. I was a quiet sort of person there, as well. I also stayed home a lot there, too. Back there, it was because there was so much fighting in the streets and so I have learned never to go

Even though he says that the United States is now his home country, Mohammed will always call himself Afghan.

out of the house unless I have to. I try to go out more now I am here, but just find I can't sometimes.

I still think of myself as Afghan, even though I am in America. When I am with Afghan people, *I speak in the old language and do the kinds of things I used to do when I lived in Afghanistan. And when I am with white people, I kind of do the same things that they do."*

Mohammed's mother usually cooks traditional Afghan meals for the family.

MAINTAINING A DUAL IDENTITY

For some refugees, it can be a struggle to balance their original culture with the way of life in their new country. Yet, for many, this dual identity is something of which to be proud. Many Afghan refugees living in the United States call themselves Afghan Americans, and in some parts of the United States there are Afghan communities, areas where a number of Afghan families have settled together. In these places, Afghan culture is celebrated and allowed to flourish. Many Afghan families maintain certain traditions within the home, such as their style of cooking, the types of music to which they listen, and the festivals they celebrate.

STIGMA OF TERRORISM

Terrorists are extremists—political, religious, or both—who use violence to scare people into doing what they want. Before September 11, 2001, most people knew little about Afghanistan. After the al-Qaeda attacks on the United States, however, Afghanistan—and the fact that its ruling Taliban government served as willing hosts for al-Qaeda terrorists—became well-known as a haven for terrorists. Because of the huge influence of the media in the United States, many Americans came to associate Afghanistan with terrorism. This association affected how some people were treated after September 11. Many members of Islamic organizations and other Muslims, including Arab-Americans, were harassed by misguided Americans looking to take their anger out on someone—even though the victims were born in the United States, may not have actually been Afghan, and were themselves against terrorism.

"I don't think people treat me differently because I'm Afghan. There are plenty of other guys at my school who are Afghan, so it doesn't seem that different. My friends and I don't really talk about our different cultures that much. I feel like this is my home now—as much as I did in Afghanistan. I have other friends who are also refugees, and they've got their own stories to tell. But most of the time, my friends and I just want to play. Or we like to tell jokes and laugh about things.

I like the fact there are a lot of cultures living side-by-side. Most people are quite similar really.

I don't care what nationality a person is. I like everybody. I don't mind where they come from.

A typical day for me goes something like this: I take the bus to school with my brother and sister. When I get there, I spend my day inside the classrooms. Then, after that I come back home and do homework. That's about all I do. I spend lunchtimes with the guys—my friends. We sit together at a big table where we talk and eat and say things to each other, like, 'What have you been doing?' And when another guy has had the same class after you, he might say, 'What did you study

On Saturdays, Mohammed and his brother Mahdi catch a bus to the mosque, where they study the Qur'an.

The Nazari family is happy living in St. Louis. Mohammed describes his neighbors as friendly and the suburban streets as very quiet.

in class?' If it's an easy thing, they go to class—and if not, sometimes they skip.

I seem to spend most of my time at school. And then, when I get home, I usually have a lot of homework to do. I also help my brother and sister with their homework, although lately they have started going to after-school programs and tutoring at Kingdom House.

At home, I also help my mom with the chores, like clearing up and cooking dinner sometimes, too.

Sometimes I like to be alone, but other times I want to be with other kids when we can all talk to each other about what's been going on in our lives. It makes me happy that I have plenty of freedom to see friends and go places if I want to these days. I also like reading, too. We have a lot of books in the house."

FACTS: EMPLOYMENT FOR AFGHANS

Even for the most skilled Afghans, it is difficult to establish whether the struggle to find work is greater in their home country or in their country of asylum.

• Recently, the City University of London conducted a survey and found that only 29 percent of refugees living in the UK were employed.

• Inability to speak the languages of their new countries and lack of local work experience can put refugees at a disadvantage when seeking jobs.

• Many refugees find that their professional skills are not recognized in their new countries. Refugees trained as doctors, nurses, and teachers can find themselves working as laborers or shop assistants, if they can find work at all.

• The unemployment rate in Afghanistan is 78 percent, while in the United States, the official unemployment rate is 5.4 percent.

• Afghanistan's economy is greatly dependent on the growth and sale of opium poppies, the plants that are used to make the drug heroin.

Opium poppies, the plants from which the drug heroin is made, grow very easily in Afghanistan's hot, dry climate.

CHAPTER FIVE: Looking to the Future

Multiple losses of people, places, and possessions, combined with the culture shock of life in a new country, can be a lot for a young person to adjust to. Evidence suggests, however, that most young refugees adapt incredibly quickly to their new way of life, with the majority feeling determined to be successful in their chosen career and, generally, feeling optimistic about the future.

MOHAMMED SAYS: *"I don't really think about what I'll do when I grow up. I know I want to be a doctor and work in a hospital, although, at the moment, I also want to be a movie star.*

I would like to live in California one day. I haven't been there yet, but I have heard it's a good place as some friends of our family live there. They tell us the climate is good and that a lot of Afghans live in their neighborhood. They say it's a really good place to live.

Right now, what I really wish is that Afghanistan was the same as the U.S. is— where everybody is free. There is nothing bad about living in the U.S. It is getting to be much more free in Afghanistan than it ever used to be, though.

Mohammed hopes to travel to Germany, where much of his family now lives.

Before, the Taliban forced men to have long beards and things like that. But now that they don't have to, most men have shaved their beards off. If I were president of Afghanistan or America, I would make sure everybody in the world was free."

LEARNING THE LANGUAGE

The most important skill that most refugees need when they arrive in their new country is knowledge of the local language. Asylum

This English class is one of the many services offered to refugees by agencies such as the International Institute.

seekers and refugees settling in the UK who wish to learn English can do so for a minimal fee, while some courses run by nonprofit organizations are free. There are also organizations that provide childcare and money to cover transportation costs.

In the United States, refugees can learn English for an affordable fee through community-education classes. Some nonprofit social-service organizations offer special youth programs for young refugees. These programs include after-school language classes and homework assistance, as well as opportunities for socializing, cultural events, and help in building self-esteem.

WORK AND TRAINING PROGRAMS

Some asylum countries offer basic skills-training courses to help refugees in finding employment. Many of these courses include work-placement opportunities and mentoring programs. Young refugees often feel pressure to find employment so that they can contribute to family finances or help other family members to migrate from a strife-ridden country. Unfortunately, many refugees find that few employment opportunities are available to them in most countries today.

Basic job-training courses provide refugees with skills necessary for finding employment.

LIFE AFTER WAR

After twenty years of war, Afghanistan is slowly being rebuilt. Since the U.S.-led international coalition ended Taliban rule in 2001, the quality of life has improved for the Afghan people. The Afghan people are no longer ruled by the fundamentalist Islamic regime that was imposed by the Taliban. Children are now free to go to school; women are allowed to stop wearing the burka, if they so choose (although many still choose to wear it); and women are allowed to leave the house unaccompanied by men (although many are still harassed when they do). In spite of these, and many other, steps forward, there is still a long way to go. War has left much of Afghanistan in ruins, and it is going to take many years to recover.

During the years that the Taliban ruled Afghanistan, no girls and only a small percentage of boys were allowed to attend school.

Food is still scarce in the country because of droughts, the poor economy, and the aftermath of war. People are working hard at rebuilding their towns and cities—and their lives—but most people today in Afghanistan have to live on U.S. $1 a day.

A NEW GOVERNMENT

At the end of 2004, Hamid Karzai—the former leader of Afghanistan's interim government—became Afghanistan's first elected president. Karzai has promised his people that his government will bring peace to the war-torn nation and an end to the economy's dependence on the drug trade. Afghanistan is currently the world's leading producer of opium poppies, the plants used to make heroin. According to the United Nations, the opium trade accounts for more than 60 percent of Afghanistan's economy.

Afghanistan's new constitution has been praised by the United States. The U.N. and the United States have promised to stand by Afghanistan, helping its new government to restore peace and security to the country. The total cost of rebuilding Afghanistan is hard to calculate, but it is bound to run into billions of dollars.

At the end of 2004, Hamid Karzai was elected president of Afghanistan.

ENCOURAGED TO RETURN

Now that peace is returning to Afghanistan and the quality of life in the country is improving, the International Organization for Migration is encouraging Afghan refugees with professional skills to return to their homeland to help rebuild the country. Afghan refugees who go back to Afghanistan by choice generally qualify for the grants under the "voluntary assisted returns" package. Since the fall of the Taliban, more than three million Afghan refugees have repatriated, or returned to their native country.

AFGHAN-AMERICAN RESPONSE TO TERRORISM

The majority of Afghan-Americans condemned the al-Qaeda attacks on the United States and all subsequent acts of terrorism committed in the name of Islam around the world. Afghan-American people—because of having endured life under the Taliban themselves or being close to people who suffered under the Taliban's harsh rule—are able to understand, perhaps more than most people of the Western world, what it is like to suffer at the hands of terrorists.

MILITARY PRESENCE

Even though the U.S.-led international coalition has ended the vast majority of its military operations in Afghanistan, the United States continues to have a military presence in the country. The main reason for this is that they are still searching for Osama bin Laden and other key al-Qaeda leaders, and it is believed that these fugitives may be hiding in the mountains of Afghanistan. The U.S. government also maintains that troops must remain in Afghanistan as long as the Taliban and militant warlords remain a threat. In spite of this, there are conflicting ideas on whether the presence of U.S. forces in Afghanistan is a good thing. Some people think that Afghanistan may never stand alone until it is has the opportunity.

FACTS—AFGHANISTAN'S ONGOING NEEDS

The effort, time, and cost involved in rebuilding Afghanistan after twenty years of war are expected to be massive. Priorities include:

• Establishing effective security, including law-enforcement and justice systems, and maintaining the presence of peace-keeping forces until the country is stable enough for them to withdraw.

• Clearing away the thousands of mines scattered across the country.

• Seizing illegal guns from people around the country.

• Rebuilding roads, buildings, hospitals, and houses.

• Sowing crops and building irrigation systems for farms.

• Building water-treatment plants.

• Implementing new national education and health-care systems, and restoring the media and other vital communication systems.

• Helping people to start up companies and businesses that will increase the number of job opportunities for local people.

Many Muslims around the world, including those living in the United States at the time, were horrified by the terrorist attacks on the United States on September 11, 2001.

CHAPTER SIX: Those Who Help

Millions of refugees are currently living in exile all over the world. Some are forced to flee their homelands with no assistance. Government-funded organizations and hundreds more nongovernmental aid organizations work hard to assist desperate refugees to reach safer environments and to integrate with local communities.

The UNHCR is the official international organization responsible for overseeing all issues relating to immigration and refugees.

THE OFFICE OF THE UNITED NATIONS HIGH COMMISSIONER FOR REFUGEES

The Office of the United Nations High Commissioner for Refugees (UNHCR) was founded in 1950 by the United Nations General Assembly. The UNHCR is responsible for leading an international operation that works to protect refugees and resolve refugee problems worldwide. The organization also assists internally displaced persons, asylum seekers, and returnees (refugees who have returned to their countries of origin). The UNHCR is funded through donations, and the United States and Japan are the major donors.

RULES ABOUT REFUGEES

The 1951 Geneva Convention relating to the Status of Refugees, along with its 1967 protocol, are the main treaties outlining the rights of refugees. Although the original treaty only concerned people who had become refugees as a result of events occurring prior to January 1, 1951, the protocol extended the convention to relate to citizens of all countries. A total of 142 countries signed the Geneva Convention and a further 141 signed the Protocol. The countries that have not signed these agreements are mainly in Asia and the Middle East. In Europe, in addition to the convention relating to the status refugees, the right to asylum is guaranteed by the European Union (EU) Charter of Fundamental Rights. Many other official studies investigating the changing needs and circumstances of refugees have been conducted all over the world.

INTERNATIONAL ORGANIZATIONS

Many government-run organizations that work toward assisting refugees have influence around the world. Examples of these international organizations (IOs) include the United Nations International Children's Fund (UNICEF), UNHCR, the Economic and Social Council, the World Food Program (WFP), the Food and Agriculture Organization (FAO), and the International Committee of the Red Cross.

People entering a foreign country, including refugees, must provide documents showing their country of origin.

Many organizations have representatives in countries where people are suffering. In Afghanistan, dozens of organizations are trying to get food to people facing the threat of famine.

NONGOVERNMENTAL ORGANIZATIONS

A nongovernmental organization (NGO) is a non-profit organization of people motivated by religious values, humanitarian values, or both. These groups play a major role in providing urgently needed relief to victims of wars and natural disasters. Most NGOs employ volunteers who work "on the ground," or directly in the troubled areas, and they often provide faster and more effective results than government agencies.

THE U.S. RESETTLEMENT PROGRAM

In the United States, the government's resettlement program is a huge operation that involves many government departments. These government agencies include:

• The Immigration and Naturalization Service (INS), which determines who meets the requirements to become refugees.

• The Department of State (DOS), which arranges flights for refugees and gives funding to the NGOs that help refugees settle into the country when they first arrive.

• The Department of Health and Human Services (HHS), which supplies cash and medical assistance to arriving refugees.

43

THE BUSINESS OF HELPING PEOPLE

Dozens of nongovernmental aid organizations around the world play a significant role in assisting the UNHCR in its efforts to help refugees. Other groups—including the International Institute of St. Louis, the United States Committee for Refugees, Refugees International, the Red Cross, CARE, UNICEF, Médecins Sans Frontières (Doctors Without Borders), and the International Rescue Committee—work hard to help people in extreme situations flee to safer places.

The media also plays a big part in keeping the world informed of the plight of refugees all over the world. In addition, the media provides a way for organizations to appeal for donations from people.

A recent UK study has shown that refugee children are three times more likely to have psychological problems than nonrefugee children. This highlights the need for refugee children to receive counseling and support upon arrival to their new countries.

REFUGEES WORLDWIDE

Refugees are often forced to flee their countries because of war or a corrupt government. In these situations, people are often killed mercilessly, kidnapped, and raped, and houses and schools are often destroyed. Corrupt governments may also restrict services such as health care and keep food from needy people. Natural disasters, famines, and epidemics are other reasons for large numbers of people to leave their countries.

REFUGEE CAMPS

Some refugees manage to reach temporary accommodations in camps located in countries that neighbor the countries from which they fled. These camps, however, are not necessarily the

Refugees often find that refugee camps confront them with threats similar to those in the countries from which they fled.

safe havens they should be. They are often unequipped to deal with the numbers and needs of desperate and often traumatized refugees. Refugee camps often lack enough food or health care for the people in them.

Women and children make up most of the world's refugees and displaced persons. They flee alone or with only their children, because their husbands have either been killed, are in jail, are fighting, or have already fled or hidden. This can make women and children vulnerable to violence and sexual assault both during their journeys and in refugee camps.

RETURNING HOME

For most refugees, the ultimate resolution to their plight and what they most desire is to return to their original countries without fear. Unfortunately, a country that has endured catastrophes can take many years to rebuild and return to peace and prosperity, even with the financial assistance of other countries. Refugees returning to war-ravaged countries—such as Afghanistan—face a long road of recovery as they rebuild their lives and their beloved homelands.

HOW YOU CAN HELP

1. BE INFORMED ON THE ISSUES

From which countries are refugees fleeing and why? Watch the news on television, read newspapers, and visit the Web sites of official government and nongovernmental organizations to find out.

2. WRITE A LETTER

Write or e-mail to the UN secretary-general or your local congressperson, urging more action that helps refugees.

3. MAKE A DONATION

Consider donating some money to any official charity or aid organization. Make sure it is a registered charity. Details about how to make a donation will be included on the Web sites run by the organizations.

4. SIGN AN ONLINE PETITION

Many petitions on the Internet allow people to protest against unreasonable imprisonment of asylum seekers, poor conditions in refugee camps, and other problems faced by refugees. (Make sure the petition is on the Web site of an official organization.)

5. ARRANGE FOR A REPRESENTATIVE FROM AN ORGANIZATION TO TALK AT YOUR SCHOOL

Listening to a speaker from an organization that works with refugees makes people aware of the problems refugees face.

6. VOLUNTEER

Many organizations are grateful for volunteer workers. Check Web sites for details.

7. ORGANIZE A FUNDRAISER

With the help of an adult, arrange an event to raise money that will be donated to help refugees. Some organizations might provide you with flyers and other support materials.

Glossary

AL-QAEDA An international terrorist organization that uses of violence with the goal creating fundamentalist Islamic governments and killing people it regards as enemies of its views.

ASYLUM Protection granted by a country to someone who has been forced to become a refugee.

ASYLUM SEEKER A refugee who has applied for asylum but is waiting to hear whether he or she will be admitted to a country that accepts refugees.

BURKA A loose garment worn in public by many Afghan women that covers the entire body and face.

COUP A sudden seizing of power from a government.

CULTURE SHOCK The feeling of confusion and isolation a person may have when coming into contact to a new way of life in a new country.

DISCRIMINATION Judgment based on prejudices.

DUAL IDENTITY Having two different cultures both as one's own.

ETHNIC Relating to religion, race, culture, or nationality.

EXILE The state of being forced to live away from one's own country.

FAMINE Drastic shortage of food affecting a wide area.

IMMIGRANT A person who leaves one country to settle in another.

INFRASTRUCTURE The basic facilities, services, and systems necessary for the functioning of a country, state, or region.

INTERNALLY DISPLACED PERSONS People who have been driven from their homes due to conflict or persecution but who remain within the borders of their country.

ISLAM The religion that worships a single god, called Allah, and accepts Muhammad as Allah's last prophet.

ISLAMIST A person who believes that nations should be governed according to a strict version of Islamic law.

MENTORING PROGRAMS Social-service programs that assist people by teaching them new skills that will help them function better in a society.

MILITANT Engaged in or advocating war.

MOSQUE A Muslim place of worship.

MUJAHIDEEN Muslim military fighters.

MUSLIM A person who belongs to the Islamic religious faith.

NORTHERN ALLIANCE The political and military group in Afghanistan who practiced who opposed the Taliban and practice a more liberal form of Islam.

OPPRESSION Harsh, cruel, and controlling rule.

ORTHODOX Devoted to strict practice of traditions, especially in religion.

PERSECUTION Punishment or harassment because of race, ethnic group, gender, or politics.

PREJUDICE Dislike or negative opinion formed without any actual experience or knowledge.

QUR'AN The sacred text of Islam, believed by Muslims to contain the words of Allah as revealed to the prophet, Muhammad.

REFUGEE A person who has been forced to leave his or her country and seek shelter in another country.

SANCTUARY A safe place.

SHIITE (SHIA) A Muslim who believes that Islamic leaders should come from Muhammad's family.

STIGMA A negative association attached to something.

SUNNI A Muslim who accepts the first four Islamic leaders as Muhammad's rightful successors.

TALIBAN The militant Islamist group that took over Afghanistan in 1996 and ruled until 2001.

TERRORISM Use of force or violence by a political group whose intent is to scare or intimidate people into submitting to them.

UNITED NATIONS An international organization founded in 1945 to promote and uphold international security and peace between nations

VILIFICATION The making of statements intended to present someone or something as a cause of problems or evils.

Further Information

AMNESTY INTERNATIONAL

Amnesty International is the world's largest organization that actively campaigns for human rights. Its search engine gives access to articles on the problems facing refugees.
www.amnesty.org

HUMAN RIGHTS WATCH (HRW)

This international group of lawyers, journalists, teachers, and others investigates human rights violations. Its work has involved reporting abuses in Kosovo and working to ban landmines.
www.hrw.org

INTERNATIONAL COMMITTEE OF THE RED CROSS

The Red Cross directs and coordinates international relief activities and works to protect and provide assistance to victims of war and violence.
www.icrc.org

INTERNATIONAL INSTITUTE

An organization that helps immigrants and refugees gain independence by learning English, finding employment, gaining access to social services, and adjusting to a new way of life.
www.intlinst.org

REFUGEES INTERNATIONAL

This organization works to protect refugees and displaced people around the world. Advocates meet with refugees to learn what problems they are having and work to develop quick solutions.
www.refintl.org

THE OFFICE OF THE UNITED NATIONS HIGH COMMISSIONER FOR REFUGEES (UNHCR)

The UNHCR was established by the United Nations General Assembly in 1950. It leads and coordinates worldwide protection for refugees and helps to resolve their international conflicts. UNHCR pays particular attention to meeting the needs of children and ensuring equal rights for women and girls.
www.unhcr.ch

UNITED NATIONS' CHILDREN'S FUND (UNICEF)

UNICEF works to help children around the world through promoting immunization, the benefit of healthy food, and access to safe drinking water.
www.unicef.org

UNITED STATES COMMITTEE FOR REFUGEES AND IMMIGRANTS

Since 1911, this organization has protected the rights of refugees by improving public policy, providing professional services, and helping refugees participate in their new surroundings.
www.refugees.org

Index